AFRICA

By Tracy Vonder Brink

A Crabtree Crown Book

Crabtree Publishing
crabtreebooks.com

School-to-Home Support for Caregivers and Teachers

This appealing book is designed to teach students about core subject areas. Students will build upon what they already know about the subject, and engage in topics that they want to learn more about. Here are a few guiding questions to help readers build their comprehensions skills. Possible answers appear here in red.

Before Reading:

What do I know about Africa?

- *I know Africa is a continent.*
- *I know giraffes live in Africa.*

What do I want to learn about this topic?

- *I want to know how many countries are in Africa.*
- *I want to learn about animals that live in Africa.*

During Reading:

I'm curious to know...

- *I'm curious to know what kind of foods Africans eat.*
- *I'm curious to know what sports Africans enjoy.*

How is this like something I already know?

- *I know what foods people who live near me eat.*
- *I know what sports I like to play.*

After Reading:

What was the author trying to teach me?

- *The author was trying to teach me what kinds of landforms Africa has.*
- *The author was trying to teach me about African countries.*

How did the photographs and captions help me understand more?

- *The photographs helped me picture Africa.*
- *The captions gave me extra information.*

TABLE OF CONTENTS

CHAPTER 1
GET TO KNOW AFRICA

What continent has one of the longest rivers in the world? Where do elephants roam and hyenas hunt? Where do more than 1 billion people live?

Africa!

Half of Africa is north of the **equator**. The other half is south of the equator. Most of the continent lies in a **tropical** region.

The world has seven continents. Africa is the second largest.

OCEANS AND ISLANDS

Water surrounds almost all of Africa. The Indian Ocean and the Red Sea splash against its east. The Atlantic Ocean **borders** its west. The Mediterranean Sea washes up along its north. The Atlantic Ocean and the Indian Ocean meet at its southern tip.

More than 100 kinds of lemurs live on Madagascar. Lemurs are found nowhere else in the world.

Africa has many islands, big and small. Madagascar is one of the largest islands in the world. Seychelles is a group of small islands off Africa's eastern coast. Fishermen live on Migingo Island in Lake Victoria. Migingo is about half the size of a soccer field.

CHAPTER 2
LANDFORMS AND CLIMATE

Africa has many different types of land. Hot, dry deserts cover parts of northern and southern Africa. Grassy **plains** stretch through the continent's middle. Rain forests lie along the equator. Mountains and hills rise in the east. Africa also has lakes and rivers.

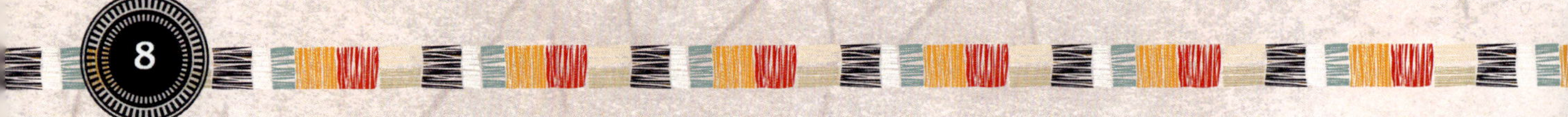

Mount Kilimanjaro rises above the savanna. It is Africa's tallest mountain. It was once an active volcano.

PLAINS

Plains, called savannas, cover almost half of Africa. Savannas near the rain forest have grass and some trees. The Serengeti plains are almost all grass. The Serengeti has a large national park and protected areas for animals.

DESERTS

The Sahara Desert covers nearly all of northern Africa. It is the largest non-polar desert in the world. The Sahara is both sand and rock. The sandy Kalahari Desert is in the south. The Namib Desert lies along the southwestern coast. It is the world's oldest desert.

Sand dunes are hills of sand piled up by desert winds.

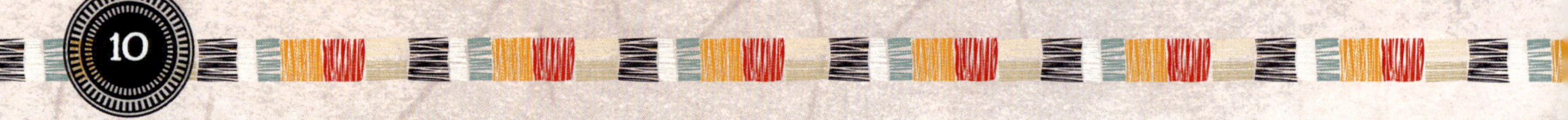

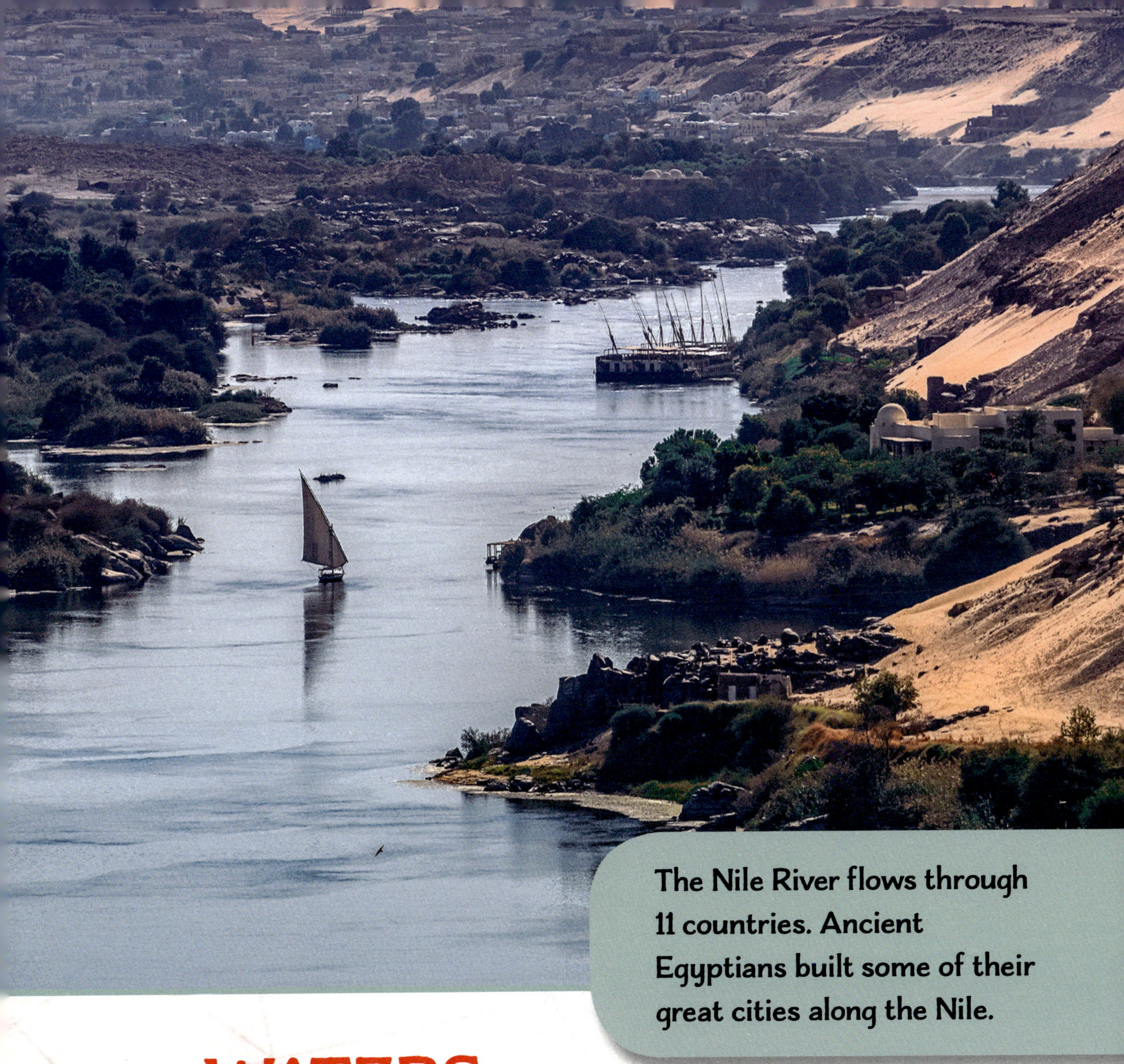

The Nile River flows through 11 countries. Ancient Egyptians built some of their great cities along the Nile.

WATERS

The Nile River is one of the longest rivers in the world. It flows from south to north through eastern Africa. The Congo is another major African river. The continent also has big lakes. Lake Victoria is the largest lake in Africa. It is also the second-largest lake in the world.

CLIMATE

Africa's **climate** is as different as its land. Much of the continent stays warm or hot all year. The rain forest zone near the equator is tropical and wet. The savanna is tropical, but it is both wet and dry. Rain can fall nearly every day in the savanna's rainy season. But very little rain falls during its dry season.

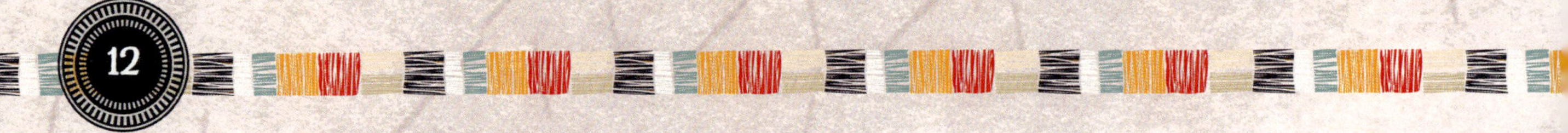

The desert zones in the north and the south have little to no rain. Summers are hot, but winters may be cool. Strong winds blow across the deserts in the spring and summer.

Every year winds blow millions of tons of dust out of North Africa. The winds may carry this dust as far away as North America.

CHAPTER 3

NATURAL RESOURCES

Africa has many valuable **minerals**. About half of the world's diamonds come from Africa. The continent produces many tons of gold every year. Metals such as copper and tin are also found there. Africa has coal, oil, and natural gas. These are sold around the world as sources of energy and fuel.

Flakes of gold can sometimes be found in streams and rivers.

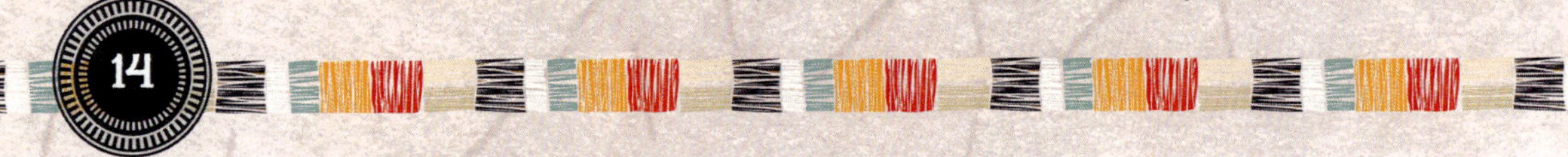

Cocoa beans come from inside the fruit of cacao trees.

Many people who live in the countryside have farms. Some crops grown in Africa are sold to other countries. The continent sends fruits, nuts, coffee, and tea around the world. West African countries supply 70% of the world's cocoa beans. Cocoa beans are the main ingredient in chocolate.

CHAPTER 4
PLANTS AND ANIMALS

Baobabs are known as "the tree of life." Some are more than 1,000 years old.

More than 20,000 different types of orchids grow in South Africa.

PLANTS

Many plants are suited to life in Africa. Acacia trees do well where the climate is hot and dry.

Baobab trees grow in low-lying areas. Baobabs store water in their trunks. They may grow to be very old.

African violets grow in the mountains of East Africa. Impatiens first grew in the same mountains. Now impatiens are used in flowerbeds around the world. Orchids bloom in forests and in the savanna.

ANIMALS OF THE RAIN FOREST

Gorillas, chimpanzees, and bonobos live in the rain forests of West Africa and Central Africa. But the forests they live in are cut down for wood or cleared for farms. Some of these animals are also hunted. These animals are **endangered**.

A conservation area is land set aside to help protect plants and animals. West Africa has nearly 2,000 protected areas.

Ostriches live in the savanna. They are the world's largest bird. They cannot fly.

ANIMALS OF THE SAVANNA

The African savanna has more **species** of hoofed **mammals** than any other continent. Elephants, the world's largest land animals, live there. Giraffes also make their homes in the savanna. They are the world's tallest animals. Antelope and zebra roam in herds through the grasslands. Many different kinds of birds are also found there.

Predators hunt in the savanna. Lions, cheetahs, leopards, and hyenas all live there. The poisonous black mamba snake also slithers through the savanna. Nile crocodiles live in rivers and swamps.

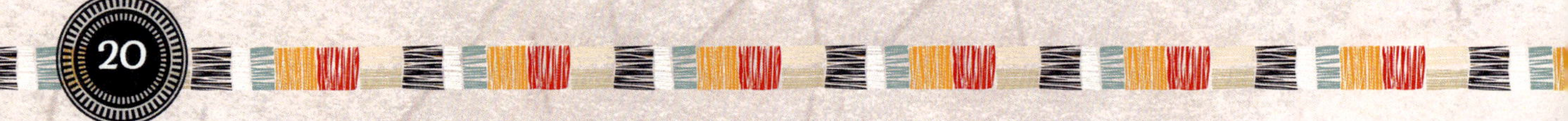

FISH

Africa has some unique fish. The lungfish lives in water, but it breathes air. Electric catfish can shock enemies and zap prey. Great white sharks hunt along the South African coast.

The largest great white shark tagged off South Africa's coast was more than 16 feet (5 m) long.

CHAPTER 5
COUNTRIES AND CITIES

COUNTRIES

Africa has 54 countries. Forty-eight are on the continent's mainland, and 6 are island nations. Most African countries are governed by elected leaders. Three countries are ruled by kings.

The Paramount King and the Queen Mother are joined by others during a festival procession under a royal umbrella in Ghana, West Africa.

Algeria has the most land of any African country. Nigeria has the most people. More than 200 million people live there. Seychelles is Africa's smallest country. About 99,000 people have homes on the Seychelles islands.

CITIES

About half of Africa's people live in small villages or farms in the countryside. The continent also has large cities. Lagos, Nigeria, is Africa's largest city. Cairo, Egypt, is another large city. Cities grow quickly as people move there from the countryside. In some countries, more people live in cities than in the countryside.

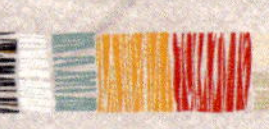

Life in an African city is like any other big city. People live in apartments, go to work, and shop at supermarkets. But some people in cities are poor. They may have no power or running water.

CHAPTER 6

CULTURE AND PEOPLE

Human life began in Africa between six and two million years ago. That is why Africa is sometimes called the Cradle of Humankind. Africa is also known for the great civilization of ancient Egypt. Its pyramids date back more than 4,000 years.

For more than 300 years, Europeans and Americans sent ships to capture and enslave African people. Around 12.5 million Africans were taken from their homes and forced to live and work on other continents.

The Maasai have lived in East Africa for hundreds of years. They are herders who raise cattle, goats, and sheep.

Nearly 2,000 different languages are spoken in Africa. Several thousand different cultural groups live on the continent. Many have their own traditions. The Maasai people live in the countryside in much the same way as their ancestors did.

FOODS

Many African countries have favorite foods. Nigerians enjoy smoky-tasting jollof rice served with meat. South Africans love spicy peri peri chicken. Ethiopians scoop up stew with a flatbread called injera.

The African Cup of Nations is the most important soccer tournament in Africa.

SPORTS

Sports are enjoyed throughout Africa. Runners from Kenya won gold medals in the 2020 Olympics. Basketball is also popular. But soccer is Africa's favorite sport.

GLOSSARY

border (BOR-dr): The place where one area ends and another starts

climate (KLAI-muht): The usual weather conditions in a certain region or area

endangered (in-DAYN-jrd): In danger of dying off

equator (EE-kway-tr): An imaginary line around the middle of Earth that is the same distance from the North Pole to the South Pole

mammal (MA-muhl): A warm-blooded animal that has a backbone, grows hair or fur, and the mother produces milk to feed her young

plains (PLAYNZ): A large stretch of mostly flat land

predator (PREH-duh-tr): An animal that lives by killing and eating other animals

species (SPEE-sheez or SPEE-sees): A group of animals or plants that are alike in certain ways

tropical (TRAH-puh-kl): Of or having to do with the part of the world near the equator where the weather is very warm

INDEX

COMPREHENSION QUESTIONS

1. How many people live in Africa?

   a. Fewer than 2 million

   b. About 100 million

   c. More than 1 billion

2. Which animal lives in the African rain forests?

   a. Gorilla

   b. Antelope

   c. Giraffe

3. What African country has the most people?

   a. Seychelles

   b. Nigeria

   c. Algeria

4. True or False: All of Africa lies below the equator.

5. True of False: Savannas cover all of Africa.

Answers: 1. C, 2. A, 3. B, 4. False, 5. False

ABOUT THE AUTHOR

Tracy Vonder Brink loves true stories and facts. She has written more than 20 books for kids and is a contributing editor for three children's science magazines. Tracy lives in Cincinnati, Ohio, with her husband, two daughters, and two rescue dogs.

Crabtree Publishing

crabtreebooks.com 800-387-7650

In Canada: We acknowledge the financial support of the Government of Canada through the Canada Book Fund for our publishing activities.

Written by: Tracy Vonder Brink
Cover design by: Kathy Walsh
Interior design by: Kathy Walsh
Series Development: James Earley
Proofreader: Crystal Sikkens
Educational Consultant: Marie Lemke M.Ed.
Print coordinator: Katherine Kantor

Hardcover	978-1-0396-6050-2
Paperback	978-1-0396-6245-2
Ebook (pdf)	978-1-0396-7041-9
Epub	978-1-0396-7239-0
Read-along	978-1-0396-7437-0

Printed in Canada/022024/CP20240215

Library and Archives Canada Cataloguing in Publication
Title: Africa / by Tracy Vonder Brink.
Names: Vonder Brink, Tracy, author.
Description: Series statement: Seven continents of the world | "A Crabtree Crown book". | Includes index.
Identifiers: Canadiana (print) 20220422397 | Canadiana (ebook) 202204223400 | ISBN 9781039660502 (hardcover) | ISBN 9781039662452 (softcover) | ISBN 9781039670419 (PDF) | ISBN 9781039672390 (EPUB) | ISBN 9781039674370 (read-along ebook)
Subjects: LCSH: Africa—Geography—Juvenile literature. | LCSH: Africa—Juvenile literature.
Classification: LCC DT6.7 .V66 2023 | DDC j916—dc23

Published in Canada
Crabtree Publishing
616 Welland Avenue
St. Catharines, Ontario
L2M 5V6

Published in the United States
Crabtree Publishing
347 Fifth Avenue
Suite 1402-145
New York, NY 10016

Photographs: Shutterstock; Cover: ©Triff, ©Khurasan, ©nypl, @Dima_designer, ©Onyx9; Title Pg: ©Triff, ©Dima_designer; Pg 3-32: ©Triff; Pg 4-31: ©lolya1988, ©Leonova Elena; Pg 4: ©hansen.matthew.d; Pg 6: ©Konoplytska; Pg 7; ©Dirk Daniel Mann, ©Volina; Pg 8: ©gdvcom; Pg 9: ©Anna Om; Pg 10: Dietmar Temps; Pg 11: ©leshiy985; Pg 12: ©Travel Stock; Pg 13: ©Purpurink; Pg 14: ©Pierre-Yves Babelon; Pg 15: ©matteoguedia; Pg 16: ©KENTA SUDO; Pg 17: ©MyTravel Curator; Pg 18: ©Chris Humphries; Pg 19: ©EcoPrint; Pg 20: ©Volodymyr Burdiak; Pg 21: ©Sergey Uryadnikov; Pg 22: ©Rainer Lesniewski; Pg 23: ©James Dalrymple; Pg 24: ©Pecold; Pg 25: ©AlexAnton; Pg 26: ©Gurgen Bakhshetyan; Pg 27: ©ebonyeg; Pg 28: © Ezume Images; Pg 29: ©mohsen nabil

Library of Congress Cataloging-in-Publication Data
Names: Vonder Brink, Tracy, author.
Title: Africa / by Tracy Vonder Brink.
Description: [New York] : Crabtree Publishing Company, [2023] | Series: Seven continents of the world | "A Crabtree Crown book."
Identifiers: LCCN 2022041796 (print) | LCCN 2022041797 (ebook) | ISBN 9781039660502 (hardcover) | ISBN 9781039662452 (paperback) | ISBN 9781039670419 (ebook) | ISBN 9781039672390 (epub) | ISBN 9781039674370
Subjects: LCSH: Africa--Geography--Juvenile literature.
Classification: LCC DT6.7 .V663 2023 (print) | LCC DT6.7 (ebook) | DDC 916.04--dc23/eng/20220901
LC record available at https://lccn.loc.gov/2022041796
LC ebook record available at https://lccn.loc.gov/2022041797